Crow Impressions
& Other Poems

The cover illustration, "Woven Together," is from a woodcut on a skateboard deck by Ryan Livingstone, 2015. It was created for an art auction held to raise funds in support of a new skatepark in Fredericton, New Brunswick dedicated to the memory of Isaac William Miller, grandson of Edith Miller.

CROW IMPRESSIONS
& OTHER POEMS

EDITH HOISINGTON MILLER

CHAPEL STREET EDITIONS

Copyright © 2016 Edith Hoisington Miller

Published by
Chapel Street Editions
150 Chapel Street
Woodstock, NB Canada E7M 1H4

www.chapelstreeteditions.com

Library and Archives Canada Cataloguing in Publication

Miller, Edith Hoisington
[Poems. Selections]
    Crow impressions & other poems / Edith Hoisington Miller.

ISBN 978-1-988299-01-3 (paperback)

    I. Title. II. Title: Crow impressions and other poems.

PS8626.I4475A6 2016   C811'.6   C2016-903070-9

Book design by Brendan Helmuth

The text is set in Myriad Pro, a humanist sans-serif typeface designed by Robert Slimbach and Carol Twombly for Adobe Systems.

The cover illustration, "Woven Together," is from a woodcut on a skateboard deck by Ryan Livingstone, 2015.

Dedication

For my husband, Michael R. Miller, a master of music, including choral works I have enjoyed singing. He has been a loving helpmeet for over fifty years. He has let me breathe.

Contents

Acknowledgements i
Foreword iii
Eight Crow Impressions 1
Other Animals 11
    Cock Pheasant 13
    Pigeons 15
    Singers. 16
    Seagulls 17
    Squirrels. 18
    Turtle. 19
    Cat Haiku 20
    Cat 21
    Toad 23
Play 25
    Barber Shop 27
    Hard Hats 29
    QWERTY, With Certainty 30
    Pan's Pipes 32
    Come To My Senses 33
Waterways 37
    Brook. 39
    Ocean 42
    Long Island Sound 44
    Quarry Pool. 46
    Tidal Bore. 47
    Tantramar 51

Six Links To the Past 55
    Kachina 57
    Living Link 58
    Revisiting New Brunswick History. 59
    Crossing a Time Space 60
    No Adventure Better 61
    Air Shaft 63

Mysteries 69
    Fundy Enigma 71
    Webs 73
    Moqui Arizona 75
    Spirit 79
    Mysterious Openings. 82
    Meeting Together 84

Ram Island Memories 89
    Morning on Ram Island 91
    Osprey. 93
    Eaglets. 94
    Herons 95
    Bay Blast 97

Dedications. 99
    Big Bang Theory 101
    Different Strokes. 103
    For Liv, At Ten Months 105
    Six Elegies For Isaac 106

Notes 115
About the Author 119

Acknowledgements

I was honoured when Harry Thurston agreed to sit down with me in 1994 to critique my less than half dozen poems, starting with "Cock Pheasant" and the first of "Crow Impressions."

My grandmother, May Folwell Hoisington, was a notable poet in the early 20th century until the 1940s. Although, as a young person, I lacked interest in her work, perhaps I have inherited some of her influence.

My New York City pal, William Hodson Mogan, a writer and editor at McGraw-Hill Book Company, was the biggest influence on and critic of my writing.

I thank Keith Helmuth for his willingness to enable my innermost thoughts and experiences to be heard by many others through his publishing, and am grateful for his insightful editing.

Foreword

Welcome to the poetry of Edith Hoisington Miller. Through her book, *Crow Impressions & Other Poems*, we travel through Edith Miller's life, a journey lived to the fullest through family stories, travel adventures, nature, music, and history. In her poetry, we discover a writer who has spent her life as a quiet observer, but, at the same time, deeply engaged in natural and cultural environments. Her poems carry the themes of her existence, from one to the other, none more important than another, all presented in clear, sharp images.

Birds are her messengers, especially crows. She begins and ends her journey with crows. The poet is strong in the belief that spirit is demonstrated through her association with crows. They journey with her as a metaphor for her respect for all beings.

Although Edith Miller has been a writer all her life, the move to poetry has come in recent years. This collection, however, has clearly been a lifetime in the making. She humbly reaches back to age seven and includes her first poem, which begins; "I have a little toad / And he walks on the road…" This poem, from the heart of a child, is early evidence of the author's care for Earth's creatures and predicts how she will bring years of experience and the power of her words into poetic expression.

The poetry changes tempo midway through the narrative as music filters through the ebb and flow. The poet's spirit rises to a new beat, a different rhythm. The theme of her life unfolds in the poem, "Meeting Together." In this poem, she describes her passion, working for Peace, Justice, and Right Relationship with Mother Earth. She brings her book to a conclusion with six brave and touching elegies for a grandson, lost at age fourteen. In this thoughtful collection of poetry, Edith Miller details her engagement with the beauty of the world and shares her firm hold on the joys of living. Enjoy the journey.

Thelma Ann Brennan
Johnville, New Brunswick

Thelma Ann Brennan is the author of a biography, *The Real Klondike Kate*, a novel of Irish/Canadian history, *The Hawthorne Bush*, and a recent volume of poetry, *Earth Carries Spirit*. She was a founding member of the Writers' Federation of New Brunswick.

Eight Crow Impressions

1

Hopping into a tree,
Springing
As if from one tiny trampoline
To another, onto a branch,
And pausing,
The crow preens:
Streamlined, sleek,
Its body a versatile black,
Soft in dull light,
Glossy in the bright.
It commences to clean its beak,
Sharpens it on a limb,
A knife on a carborundum,
Fences with it, parries,
Probes under an uplifted wing.
Hold fast this impression,
A spirit sign,
Before the messenger answers
The caw of a companion
And whips off.

2

A man, gripping a shotgun,
Steals through the grass,
Stops at the caw and looks up
To the finial tip of a larch,
Unbent under the crow.
No matter that the fable called
The crow's voice cursed,
The man laughs at its rasp,
Mimics it, contests it, and
Strides home, his gun lopped in his hand.

3

Was it a sandpiper or heron?
A steady dart, it sailed
Past my window,
Wings in measured pumping,
Long prow pointing.
But it was really a crow,
Its bill extended by a stick,
Secured for the route to the nest.

4

A lone Sparrow
Pecks the porch floor,
Hops to the windowpane,
Eyes my face
At the curtain's edge.

Three crows
Arrive with fanfare,
But flash off, vociferously,
As if vexed
At the human hint.

5

A clan of crows –
I counted 26 – reunited
At their spring place,
Hailing one another
With signal caws and cackles.

Crashing into the tops
Of the tallest trees on the street,
On spindle tips of larch and
Splayed crowns of spruce,
They settled in the sky.

6

In the middle of the winter night
I awake to a clamour of crows
Clustered on the pine windbreak.
Hundreds of amassed crows
Lust for community.
A crow's individual voice is lost
In a pointillism of caws and mewls,
A jubilant soundscape
Of a crow society reunion
For the common crow good.

7

A carpet of crow-speak
Greets the first light.
Spread out on the flattened cornfield
They glean the harvester's spilled corn.
Then gulls drop in.
A black and white patchwork,
Gulls join in the crows'
Fused cacophony.
The convention of birds
Feast in the field of babel.

8

I heard a mooing at first light.
But how could it be a cow?
The farmer next door
Had no cows on his field.
It sounded like a cow in miniature.
There was a rustle and then a moo.
It must have been a predator
Disturbing a crow or raven from its sleep.

Other Animals

Cock Pheasant

A long string in the fresh snow,
Cock pheasant tracks
Bypass the hidden seed pile,
But the next day
Tracks radiate from the pile.
On the third day he hammers at it,
His feral eye matches my eyes at the window.

Dull weather browns his body
But in the sun, colors emerge endlessly,
Multi-elemental:
Burnished copper and Atahualpa's gold,
Emerald and aquamarine stone,
Sleek ice and soft black sealskin,
Rival of the peacock and patterned butterfly.

He is a stunning strutter,
His wattles engorged, flared scarlet.
If the hens aren't impressed
By his long tail,
Pushed into a right angle
By goldenrod stalks,
The red rut cannot be ignored.

Now uniformed in Eton collar and red insignia,
He postures, alert over his hens'
Staccato peckings at the seed,
His warning crow punctuates
The air acres away,
His brandishing wings vibrate
Through insulated walls.

Pigeons

Above detritus pigeons strut
In dust, extract edibles, and
Make their homes on ledges
Behind screens and spikes, as
On park patchwork.
They step like
Old silent newsreels of
Men in top hats and cutaways,
Soldiers and honour guards, and –
with Chaplin eloquence – dancers.
They court, concentrate and
Economically dodge human legs.
He bows and wheels around,
Sidles up to her as she
Turns away a fraction.
As if to an unheard caller,
They repeat their choreography,
Their rite of all seasons,
In perpetual elegance,
On hard sidewalk.

Singers

The song sparrow sings for a mate
From the peak of his
Rosebush podium.
His voice bursts forth,
Resounds into open windows.
He tests his talents;
Repeats phrases yet
Ripples improvisations
That impress the she-sparrow.

The soprano sings an aria,
Her voice, released into
Fine church acoustics,
From apse to arches,
Soars glorious, jubilant.
And together with the trumpeter
Perform a perfect duet,
As close as love-makers
When in love.

Seagulls

A seagull flies alongside a ship
At the same speed and
Eye level as mine on deck.
As our eyes meet,
His twitches a little in
A kind of recognition.

He falls behind and
Keels over, like
A banking airplane,
Breaks the glide, and
Furiously flaps away
To join his kin.

Squirrels

Two squirrels circle a tree.
Like two spotlights playing
In the dark to music, and
Like staccato notes,
Urgent and quick,
They stop to mate.

They resume their chase,
Dart around the bark,
Peek and meet
As in peekaboo play, and
In a downward spiral,
They dash to earth.

Turtle

Poor turtle:
How I have neglected her.
As I watch birds and bees flit,
She cruises her water
In solitude.

Mourning turtle:
When her sister became sick
She sensed something wrong
And soon after, her sister
Floated dead.

Hungry turtle:
In a search for food she glides
And neatly seizes a pellet.
I can hear her beak
Across the room: Snap!

Turtle at rest:
She labours up the rock slab
To pose at last in the sun,
Stretches out splayed claws
Like in an arabesque.

Shedding turtle:
As her shell contracts
The scutes spring from it,
And each scruffy curl reveals
Fresh shell, renewed turtle.

Cat Haiku

O Sphynx-cat, contemplate,
Guard your peace while you can;
A flea is coming.

Cat

I think of my cat with the letter "S" –
Her very name, Zsazsa, slithers.
She comes on little feet like fog,
Like strokes of velvet,
Soft as powder,
Subtle and dainty, even her meow
A truncated "me–!"

Ears like a silk purse,
Whiskers magnificent as
Dew on a morning cobweb
Or frost on winter twigs,
She purrs, insinuates herself,
Glides her fur across my leg,
Touches a wet nose to my toes.

Add to this the sound of "C" –
A captivating study of constant grooming,
She keeps clean her royal coat
Of lustrous sheen with
Tireless tongue between
Splayed claws and who knows
Where she will wash next.

From being sedentary puss to
Predator readying her haunches,
She calculates killing a chipmunk.
After the birds take flight, and
A feral Tom slinks away,
The chipmunk catch is found
Draped over the doormat.

What an acrobat she is,
With a spatial sense,
She can leap tall sills
In a single bound.
Suddenly she drops down,
Seeks company,
Crosses the bridge of my legs,
Cuddles in my lap,
Casts alluring eyes at me,
Invites caresses,
Speaks to me in silence.
Does she crave love?
Is she capable of love?
We communicate.

Toad

    I have a little toad
And he walks on the road
      And on the water.
     He rides in a boat,
    A little carved boat.

– first poem, age seven

Play

Barber Shop

With shears and comb crossed,
The barber cuts
Measured lengths.
Customers sense a sureness,
Become solemn, centered, in

The sanctity of the room.
A customer seeks out his oracle,
Sounds out on politics and plans
Of the town gone awry
With wasteful spending.
Waiting wives grin as

Men's talk hangs in the air.
An old sidewalk philosopher
Comes in and sits in his corner,
Carries the topic further,
Adds his opinion,
Adjusts his old fedora,

And thumbs through a newspaper.
The barber evaluates his work:
His whisk of baby-brush softness
Comforts the customer's neck.
Wisps, increasingly minced,
Fall to the fluffed floor of

Mounded multicoloured hair.
Shears, razor, and comb alternate
As he keeps his pace,
Creates new shape.
The barber's sculpture
Is a testament to
The sanctity of the room.

Hard Hats

As soldiers salute,
Olive for war, blue for peace,
A death-dropped helmet
Rolls like a skull.

Queen, Premier, and workers
Grin at their uniform yellow dome.
Ready now, the PR person
Guides the factory tour.

An upturned hockey helmet
On a shelf invites,
Receives the cat, where she
Nests in a hermit crab curl.

The classic black helmet,
Plush like a caribou's horn,
An equestrian icon,
Crowns blue jeans and sneakers.

Head encased in a pink globe,
Like a deep-sea diver,
A little Barbie
Rides her pink training bike.

QWERTY, With Certainty

A picture of an old typewriter startles me,
Surprises my computer complacency.
A block of naked machinery,
Its black and gold glosses through the newsprint.
My senses are prickling.

I can smell a sour mix
Of metal, oil, alcohol in the air.
Every time old Mr. Jones the repairman left,
I wondered if it was the cleaning fluid
Or if he'd been drinking.

I can feel my fingertips tracing
Each pad that fits into a rimmed,
Round key with a Roman letter
Capped by celluloid, on top of
A metal stem, trembling.

I can hear the clacking
Of metal on crisp paper,
The carriage smashing across the machine.
Stabilized by rubber feet,
It's not wavering.

I can see myself tapping
On my first journal at age seven,
"Flash the Morning News."
I am searching for the right letter
On the keyboard, learning.

I can still read the non-decaying
Paper, kept intact by rag content.
Its lists of pets, riddles,
News and commentary,
Keep me laughing.

The typewriter organ is surviving,
Has moulted its metal, changed its works
From the mechanical to the electronic, but
QWERTY, with certainty, remains
A keyboard layout unchanging.

Pan's Pipes

On a walk with my husband and sons,
I came to the foundation of
An old farmhouse
Surrounded by a harvested field
Covered with grain stalks,

Rigid stubs,
Short and sharp;
Hard, cut-off, hollow stems
In rows of even height.

I picked my way along, and
As I stepped on them
The hollow stalks popped in different pitches.
With glee, the boys joined in and
We stomped all over the field.

Better than snapping bubble wrap,
The straws were like panpipes.
With resonating pitches,
Pan conducted our playing his pipes
In a straw popping symphony.

Come To My Senses

I give thanks for the senses
And ponder which I would sacrifice
One for another,
If I had to.

Could I live without hearing
Bach's "B-Minor Mass,"
Michael's "Mass For Peace"
Or at his piano in "Clair de Lune,"
Joel on soprano sax in a Jewish wedding song,
Or on tenor sax in "Caravan,"
Nate's deft hands on a moon drum,
Gene Krupa in "Dark Eyes,"
Andrew's double bass in Rachmaninov's "Vocalise,"
Slam Stewart's jazz bass in "Gotta Be This Or That,"
Laotian, Romanian and Peruvian panpipes,
A song sparrow in his love serenade,
A mournful loon or raspy heron on the bay,
Even the bawl of a baby crow?

How about seeing
My favourite art works at home,
Ballet and breakdance on stage,
Woodpeckers striking the feeder,
Chipmunks in smartly striped suits
Dashing for dropped seeds,
Salamanders on a full-moon night

Slithering among the fallen leaves,
Like worms but for their dainty legs,
An eagle swooping to the road for prey, then,
Rising abruptly broad-winged in front of our car,
Adroitly flying off,
Granddaughters gracing my life –
Little Liv's Dresden-doll complexion
Framed by flames of red hair,
And Lucy and Ella
Like Rose Red and Snow White,
Radiating their individual beauty?

What about taste?
Not for me these bizarre combinations
Touted by chef shows and cookbooks,
To boost fad and marketing –
Curry and maple syrup, kale in ice cream –
Nor for me Nate's vegan diet.
I'll stick to my old-fashioned palate –
Meat 'n' taters, a bucket of KFC chicken.
But without the sense of taste
I might not over-eat,
And I could tolerate an offering of
A mayonnaise-slathered sandwich or
Raw fish and roe, to be polite.
I would not even miss bacon and eggs,
Maine fish chowder with oyster crackers,
Cracklings from my mother's roast pork,
Fresh maple sugar.

Without touch there would be no itches,
Childbirth agony, back pains,
Sore throats, anesthetics,
Though not heeding yellow jackets
Might be a problem.
But I could not delight in a dip
In the cold bay to wash off summer sweat,
The crisp air on a walk in autumn or spring,
Early winter snowflakes on my face,
A foot massage,
A cat's luxurious fur,
A love-caress.

Almost as much as ears and eyes
I would miss the sense of smell.
A balsam-fir branch as I attach a bauble,
A bay leaf when I snap it off the stem,
Salt-slapped mist of the bay,
Aroma from sweetgrass in humidity,
The field of hay for hours after mowing
At the farm next door,
The lavender sachet in my drawer,
That bouquet of freesia every anniversary,
These I would miss.
I give thanks for the senses,
Mysteriously part of
My body and soul
And still intact.

Waterways

Brook

Below the bridge over the brook,
My childhood domain,
Water-striders skated,
Water-boatmen twirled in
Placid pools between rocks,
Yellow-spotted brick-red
Efts scampered,
Tame currents babbled,
In rhythms and in sync
With mental melodies.

The brook could be calm as a spill from
A glass of water on a table
Or in a hurry on a rampage.
On the deeper side of the bridge
Downstream a waterfall fiercely hissed
Its reminder of the risk at the edge,
But the space above it was a respite,
A benign basin to bathe in.
After the border of the falls,
The brook continued, again
Too deep and forbidding,
Until it fed into a pond.

The hurricane of 1938 flooded
The bridge and area
All the way to the pond and around.

The whole swollen brook
Furiously delivered
A flotsam of branches
And oddly displaced items.
In the embrace of my family,
I explored the flood; in
Rubber boots we picked our way.

From the bridge, my balcony,
I dropped stones in the water to listen to
The echo of their plonk and splash,
Tossed sticks and leaves of
Autumn-hued maples and beeches
Into the urgent stream, and like
Kaleidoscopes they spun in eddies as
I watched the current take them and guessed
How many seconds it would take
For them to pass under and whether or where
They would bump into the banks.

Winter slowed the flow.
The iced-over pond
Was now a skating rink
For whole families,
Their members equal and free

To figure skate, play hockey, join in the whip.
But still, the brook fed the pond,
Thin ice fringed it,
Chunks dropped from the banks and
Little bergs floated in the brook.

In spring I made mud pies
Over a boulder and left them to bake,
Turned over rocks to see
Millipedes spiral themselves
In disguise as "pennies,"
Paved muddy paths with sticks
In cross-hatches and endless
Geometric designs, and
Rinsed my hands in the brook.

Across from a bog of skunk cabbage
And jack-in-the-pulpit,
I was back to the summer's play among
The rocks of the shallows and a bank of
Columbines, lady's slippers,
Ferns, and Dutchman's britches
Encircled with pebbles,
And it became a fairy park.

Ocean

I fling off my beach towel,
strip off sandals and
squoosh feet in hot sand,
hesitate at the edge of the ocean,
pretend to ignore the chill of the air,
laugh at my companions,
and confront the water,
as I brave myself for the first plunge
of the year in the Atlantic Ocean.

I could delay the immersion endlessly,
explore the sands for blanched crab shells,
marbled stones, frayed scraps of rope
and scattered pieces of buoys,
look up at gulls, terns and cormorants,
search the water for distant eider nurseries,
until the binoculars tire my eyes, but
no matter what, I need my Communion.
And so I approach the ocean,
slowly adjust myself as I dunk my
goose-bumped body in and thrash around.

Wild surf slaps me off my feet,
kicks up a stew of sand into my face,
scrambles me like a turned turtle,
turns me back to a primitive time
of sharpened senses.
Before I can decide whether
to let the next one master me or
Dive deep and go along with its undulation,
Some urge has decided for me
to jump into the next wave,
and have another wild tumble.

Long Island Sound

In my grandfather's sailboat,
"The Poco Pronto,"
I sailed with him and my family.
Not inclined to being a sailor,
I just went along for the ride,

Not worth a drop of salt water
Unless I tried to learn the ropes,
A stern captain, my grandfather
Made sure I explored the basics:
I adjusted the mainsail and jib sheets,
Lifted the centreboard through
Mussel shoals and shallows,
Steered the tiller, aimed for
A steady distant spot, but
When the boom swung around –

You'd better duck or it could
Smash into your skull –
"Ready about - hard a'lee!"
He roared and we ducked as
The sail luffed and realigned.

And then out in the middle of
The Sound we anchored,
Threw off shirts and hats and
Rolled over the gunwale into salty water
Shallow enough for me, and

Crunched onto sharp mussel shells in
Old sneakers, saved for the situation,
And swam our sweat off and
Played around like happy seals, then
Back on board we picnicked.

But my favourite spot was the bow,
A haven removed from
Sailors' nautical reckonings,
Where I lay prone and straddled the jib,
A secure fit for my size.

The wind cooled my sunburn,
The waves rinsed my face, and
Their rhythm coordinated with
Music in my head that
Sometimes lulled me to sleep.

I awakened to more captain's orders.
Grabbed my tote of thermos and sun salve,
Oars thumped on the lurching hull that
Bumped into the harbour wall,
And we tied up to the mooring.

Quarry Pool

Yes, I'm from New Jersey,
That state mocked as a kind of
Poor-man's New York City,
Unsophisticated and out in the sticks.

Yes, trees and swaths of wilderness,
North of Newark to the Appalachian Trail,
Lakes, wild and manmade,
Abandoned quarries filled with still water.

      * * * *

On a hot, brilliant day
I climbed the bank of the quarry,
Gripped crags of quartz
Loosening rocks that fell into the pool,
Their solid plops emanating echoes.

From a ledge I looked down at my target,
A sparkling ring of crystalline water, and
Jumped with a resounding *thwhomp*
Into the baptismal font.

From my frigid immersion
I popped up like a cork
Draped in splashes,
Shouted a clarion cry of joy,
Bobbed and floated in buoyant water
Under walls of clean, white stone and
Sun-blazed blue sky.

Tidal Bore

On the taut sausage-like side of a
Zodiac rubber raft I wait
With my family and other tourists
For the Tidal Bore to arrive.
I don't wear a watch –
This trip is for fun –
I leave the time-gauging to the pilot, Brian.

I crane my neck to determine
The debut of the Bore,
See uncluttered water the colour of mauve,
A special Fundy mix of ruddy water and
Blue sky, that contrasts with
The casualness of rugged woods and
Banks efficiently sculptured
To let the Bore pass freely.
The river is serene, like a lion in a long,
Restorative nap before
The spring to the kill.

Why don't I relax? I fidget,
Loosen my grip on the rope line,
Shift my position, but wonder why
We sit right on the high cheeks
Of a raft with no seat belts.
Well, I reason, the deepest part
Of the river is but two metres.
I can handle that in my safety vest and

Clown suit of yellow rubber slicker.
I mistake the approach of the Bore –
A mirage on the water,
A strip of white gypsum at the bank,
A swatch of ripples whipped up by the wind.

Is this it? My heart pounds, as indeed
The tidal wave advances,
Wriggles its sure way all along
The river's peaceful bed,
Its row of surf pushes ahead on
An insistent thirty-kilometre journey.

At precisely the right moment
Brian starts the forty-horsepower motor,
Nursed beforehand to tip-top condition,
So it roars to life with merely
One pull of the cord.
Like a white feather boa,
The Bore shivers toward us, and
Undeterred by the river banks,
Just turns up a little on them,
Like a monster with curled lips.

We zoom to meet the monster,
U-turn around it,
Ride triumphant on top of it, feel
The power of churning waves beneath us.
Like a veteran bronco rider
Brian masters the Bore, which

Pushes the river flow backwards,
That creates high, turbulent waves.
We circle back and charge into
Roller Coaster Rapids,
Plane over them, ride with them, and
The raft pitches, rolls and yaws, like
A small sailboat on the ocean.

I am lifted off my seat, a brief scare, as
A splash slaps my face, grit lines my teeth,
A puree of fine, sandy mud tinged with
A mix of salt water from the Bay of Fundy
And fresh from the river.
It's like an initiation rite, I laugh,
To taste the Tidal Bore!
We could be wetter, we could capsize,
But for the even keel and strong motor control.

A bulge in the riverbed that impedes
The rush of water creates a whirlpool.
Deceptively easy to accommodate
So we don't get sucked in,
Brian keeps us from being like a bug
Going down a bathtub drain.
The motor, so revved up against
The forceful current gives the illusion
Of traveling fast, until
We look at stationary riverbanks.

As Brian charges everywhere,
I am moment by moment surprised
That waves of a river can be as varied as
Those of a bay or ocean.
I had thought that the train of the Bore
Was tranquil, but we now ride waves
That are about three metres high.

At last the churn expires.
We cut the engine and travel a calm current
To relax and soak up the view of
Neat, orderly farms,
Bald eagles at their nest,
Black ducks harassing mallards.
A sandpiper escorts us for a while, and a few
Fishermen try their luck at shad and gaspereaux.

The waterline on the banks and
Parallel lines on sandbars tell of tide levels.
We get off to explore a mud sandbar, but
Soon the tide reminds us it has not given up,
And we hop hastily into the boat and
Follow a serene river back to the dock.
Thanks so much, I exclaim to Brian,
You satisfied my wish to have
The thrills without the worry of danger!

Tantramar

Had I landed on a different continent
When I came from an urban order
Nearly fifty years ago to
The Tantramar Marshes?
Tintamarre – the din of migrating geese.

How dull, I thought,
This flat land of grays and duns,
This scatter of little leaning hay barns on
Vast grazing fields for brown shorthorn cows,
And the brown water of the Tantramar River
Snaking all over the marshland with
Slimy mud banks, bare of plants or shells,
Continuing with its murky swill through
The gate under the highway and railroad bridge,
Feeding into the Chignecto Basin.
Yet, season by season this rich brown water
Carries a crop of gaspereau fish for the netting.

How raw, I thought,
This landscape, not realizing the need for
Some mulling and seasoning.
In the fall came a change,
A surprise among acres of tired grasses;
Blueberry fields turned to
Fiery reds tinged with mauve.
We were small figures among spacious,

Restless skyscapes of
Clouds and lightning,
Rainbows and northern lights.
Sky blue reflection on
Chignecto Basin's rust became
A Fundy mauve, and the
Tantramar River banks looked no more
Like a lifeless slime but a silken roll of
Porcelain clay caressed by a potter.

How dreary, I thought,
This marshland, until spring.
But we became explorers of new territory,
A land of dikes and their Acadian aboiteaux –
Centuries-old tidal sluices.
My family and I leaped between
Hummocks across the wetlands,
Found a perfect skull of a muskrat,
Identified the signal call of a pheasant's
Frightened clucks as I flushed it from
A bush in passing,
Discovered bobolinks flitting and
Marsh hawks soaring,
Snow buntings on our porch,
Redpolls on our driveway,
A meadowlark in Point de Bute
Overlooking High Marsh Road,
Once even a bluebird at Jolicure,

Located a bittern in spring by its boom
And spotted it past the alders across
Marshland too wet to tramp without wellies.

At Fort Beausejour we ran up to the ramparts
And rolled back down to the road,
Headed for the ancient Acadian dikes,
Some still fenced and being dredged.
We hiked their mesas overlooking
The Tantramar and Westcock Marshes.

Under winter's metallic skies,
The waterways' iridescence dulled,
Dirtied in slush and chunks
Until the persistent freeze and
Squeeze of the tides between
Slabs of rocks shaped into
Brown and white jagged ice runes,
That every day presented
A newly sculptured exhibit.

I found that nature's shapes
Mattered to me as much as its colours,
While out on the sleeping marsh hay fields
A clean cloak of whipped-cream snow
Is studded with golden wisps of grass,
And spruce on nearby slopes
Droop with silent swags of snow.

Six Links To the Past

Kachina

Some think pothunters insensitive,
Greedy robbers of graves,
And should leave the bones,
Shells and beads where they rest.
With ultrasound and electronic imaging,
Archaeologists now search for clues to
Names and dates of cultures but have lost
The visceral sense of touch,
Of hands in dirt and sherd,
Of direct connection to the past.
Is it too ephemeral to appreciate?
My Hopi kachina doll of the corn clan
Made of traditional cottonwood,
Sold to me by the artisan and legal,
Continues ancient Hopi culture,
A tangible link with their history.
No kiva or cave has been violated.

Living Link

My Inuit friend is a living link
To thousands of years of history,
Just one generation away from
A traditional fisherman, her father,
Who advised her to never forget
Their culture, their language,
Yet supported her education aims.
With one foot in the Inuit past
And the other on the modern street,
She takes along her daughter
On this seesaw of life,
Impressing on her their cultural values.
My arms around my friend can almost
Reach ten thousand years.

Revisiting New Brunswick History

At King's Landing Historical Settlement
A living history transports me
A hundred-fifty years back,
Amid the scent and haze of
Chimney smoke, haystack,
Brown bread baking,
Maple sap boiling in a cauldron,
The sound of hoof-clopping and neighing
From the horse-drawn wagon,
And the swish of women's long skirts
As they greet me with same
Old fashioned, seventeenth-century
"Good day!" I once heard
 At Plimoth Plantation in Massachusetts.

Crossing a Time Space

I wondered at those half-hidden back stairs
In my grandparents' big old
Mid-Victorian house that hinted at
Cupboards and doors to explore.
My cousins and I creaked down
An Escher-like staircase ending at a wall,
Opened a door half stuck with
A mouldy mattress spread on
The bottom flight of steps,
Entered a dark crawl space,
Like a vestige from a past life.
We stooped to explore this dank cave,
Searched for leavings, traces,
Duck-walked through droppings of
Generations of mice, and
On to the end of the gloomy space
We came to a mysterious door.
It opened to the familiar –
The laundry and furnace room,
Long ago the former kitchen
In its original lower level.
I jumped down a couple of feet
Into the sun-filled room,
Like Alice through the rabbit hole,
Like crossing a time space.

No Adventure Better

No adventure was better than
My father's exploration trips
With siblings and friends,
Not to museums or parks but
To explore vestiges of projects
Abandoned or never realized.
What remained of railroad plans,
Land dug and levelled and left trackless,
Was like the trench of an
Ancient Mound Builders site.
What once was a canal was now
A highway, sunken between
High concrete banks.
Where a railway ran parallel to it
We hiked on the tracks,
Short strides from tie to tie,
Long ones skipping ties, and
Sang to their rhythms.
It seemed that enormous sunflowers
Always grew only by train tracks,
Like an incongruous attempt
To decorate railroad apparatus,
Coal heaps and crumble of
Car-part rust among weeds –
Apt targets for stones and BBs.

This was nostalgia for my father,
A former coal salesman,
And a geography lesson for us.
Since I was not used to groomed turf
Or planned rows of flowerbeds,
I found the trips romantic.
The old canal led to a falls,
Where we waded in the cool water.

Air Shaft

First, a job in a New York ad agency,
Now, at last, an apartment in Greenwich Village
With three roommates and bunk beds –
> *the dream of a 1950s suburban girl!*

The fall chill on my neck
From the building's air shaft
Woke me up in my bottom bunk
Before the radio alarm turned on
Or the street came alive.

The heady aroma of fresh coffee
From downtown roasters
Wafted in, entrancing me
Like the smell from a fresh can
My mother would let me sniff
When she opened the seal.

The city din surrounded the building
Flowed down the air shaft with a
Distant roar like a nearby hive of bees.
Tiny whistles to walked dogs punctured the air.
Garbage trucks whined.
The shriek of a fire engine
Bursting from the station behind us
Rushed down the air shaft.

My roomies' radio turned on to
Bright-tongued chatter of weather,
News, and perky music that
Moved us out to work.
A ten-cent token took me from
The Seventh Avenue subway and
Shuttle to Madison Avenue.

I moved with the stream of commuters,
Shoes smacking and clicking on pavement,
With a dry sound or sharp after a rain,
A percussion of heel-hitting,
Making a rush-hour symphony.
After work we swapped
Tales of our day, magazine articles,
Use of the new hi-fi record player.

On the street, bag ladies and men
Stowing pickings from trashcans in
Old baby carriages and supermarket carts,
A man with a hurdy-gurdy and
Monkey collecting coins,
Real beatniks in long skirts and beads,
Long hair and beards,
Flowing robes, and leather thong sandals.
Later, I had a pair custom-made
By a leather-working artisan.

I sipped espresso in coffee houses,
Danced horas in a Polish hall,
Heard Pete Seeger and Oscar Brand,
Clapped hands to the songs of an Israeli troupe,
Frequented a club in the 18th-century house
Of Thomas Paine, now a hub
For devotés of songster-pianist Marie Blake
And her jazzy versions of "Love For Sale" and
"Mack the Knife."

On the street in front of our building
Two men with violin and guitar peddled
Traditional Neapolitan folk songs
Familiar to me from Italian-Americans
In my home town –
"O Solo Mio," "Sorrento."
I rushed to grab some money,
Tossed it into their hat.

I strolled Washington Square Park
For the Sunday music-making free-for-alls
Around the fountain/wading pool to hear
Bongos and Greek bouzoukis,
An Appalachian singer with banjo,
Even an Elvis impersonator,
Earnestly imitating the new idol.
Musical genres were somewhat sound-proofed
By the listeners packed around them.

Back in my bunk at night,
I got used to the air shaft theatre.
The couple across the wall
Clanked their glasses and cackled with
Jests and loud jokes.
The couple overhead sighed as
Their bed springs squeaked.
The film director below played
Two unfinished tunes on his piano,
Time after time.

I shopped on Christopher Street:
Broccoli from the original greengrocer
Who imported it from Italy;
Fresh fish from a rotund woman with
Tight-packed bun and black dress, who
Hauled out the catch from huge zinc vats;
Flaky croissants and brioches from a French baker;
Rye bread and bagels from a Kosher shop.

I almost bought meat from a man
Whose cat stepped over the chopped mound
Left open on the marble counter,
But instead went to Julius's,
The oldest bar in the city, garlanded with
Greasy cobwebs from decades of grill smoke,
Dusty photos of prizefighters,

Seats made from barrels,
The floor carpeted with sawdust, where
The taste of a juicy hamburger with a slab of onion
Made up for any danger-to-health suspicions.

I bade g'night, went to my room,
Nestled in my bed, and waited for the
Unseen players to recap their roles.
Smoke from a neighbourhood of
Coal furnaces and wood burning fireplaces
Crept into the air shaft.
The new scents were to me aromatic,
Somehow soothing in the brisk fall air.
With a second blanket and scarf,
My "ravelled sleeve of care" was well knit.

Mysteries

Fundy Enigma

On the Bay of Fundy,
I gazed at gulls
Cavorting in the sky, and
Down at rocks on the sand,
Some of red iron
Rounded by wave-tumble,
Some of shards of coal,

Looked for fossils of
Grasses and ferns,
Tried to extract
A fluted cane of coal from
A chunk of shale, and
Suddenly it crumbled in
My rude hand.

I was stunned,
Struck by sorrow for this
Piece of history that had lasted
Millions of years, for
An intact calamites fossil
Had just been destroyed by
My exploitive act.

Why, it's just a common fossil,
I reasoned, not a great
Work of art, or is it? I sensed
The presence of a spirit that
Claimed its artistic creation and
Judged me, yet did it
Let me off this time?

Webs

I hear a muffled buzzing.
A housefly wrestles to release itself
From a spiderweb,
Draped across the window.
A spider is alert to the catch.
Half as big as the fly, yet
Its silk veil overwhelms its prey.
If I were the size of the fly,
Would I hear it gasping for breath
Amid its frantic exercise?
Would its amplified buzz
Knock me to the floor or
Blast my eardrums?

The spider wraps its prey with
Threads around and around
Like a ball of yarn,
Like a hay-baling machine
Wrapping white plastic sheets
Around a farmer's harvest.
The spider waits for the fly to wear out,
Then neatly injects its
Proboscis into the swaddled fly,
And the creature gives up.

Will the bound prey drop onto
A web on the window sill,
Break its fall and pierce the web?
Where does the spider's diet come from:
Fruit flies, houseflies, moths?
Should I let my bananas over-ripen for
Fruit flies to materialize?

Silk filaments link items in
My natural museum on the sill –
A moon-snail shell with
A feather stabbed through
A woodpecker hole in birch bark,
Skate-egg cases with sponges, Fundy fossils,
Strand-swagged horns of a sculpture of Pan
With an ad hoc statue of copper pipe,
Cork float, lichen, Japanese bowl.

My cat leaps to the sill,
Brushes silk wisps off cactus spikes,
Makes a curl of eider-down dance,
And dust motes explode in the sunbeams.

Moqui Arizona

Moqui, an old name
But not as ancient as Hopi,
Who came from Mexico to Arizona
Over two thousand years ago,
Recorded their migrations
In different directions in petroglyphs,
Their "footprints."
They first lived in pits or cliffs,
Hunted and grew corn,
Their staple of body and spirit.
The Spaniards tried to conquer
And Christianize them,
And called them Moqui,
The Navajo and Comanche
Terrorized them, drove them
Up atop three mesas where
The Hopi hurled rocks down at them.

There the Hopi retreated and settled,
Resisted attempts by priests and pastors,
Restored their identity as Hopi –
People of peace –
And spirit in a culture of Kachinas,
Deities for the animals and plants
That affect all aspects of their lives.
They built houses of rocks with

Shale wedged in for mortar.
Here the villages still stand,
The oldest in the country, occupied
For nearly a thousand years.

On Second Mesa I learned of
The distinctive Hopi way of
Dry farming corn on arid land.
Corn is their culture,
Part of all aspects of life,
Implanted in ceremonies.
We sat down with a Hopi family,
To dine on hominy corn and mutton soup.
In a careful détente with the Navajo,
Who encroached upon Hopi land,
Even their petroglyphs,
Hopi combine corn with Navajo mutton.
Here artisans showed us their work:
A silversmith chiseled a bracelet design,
A basket maker wove a plaque of yucca
To contain blue corn, and
A potter shaped a sleek pot.

On the plaza at Third Mesa
Right where I stood,
I marveled that Hopi still practiced
Ancient Kachina dances –

Snake, deer, bear, corn, reed –
And held kiva rites, and here
I bought a pair of traditional cottonwood
Kachina dolls from the artisan.

From the height of First Mesa
I saw the same scene as in a
One-hundred-year-old photo and
Reflected on the women as they fetched water,
Balanced it in ollas on their heads, and
Hauled it back up that hill, where
Now water is piped into the plaza.
I imagined a row of women as they would
Grind corn with a mano in a metate,
And bake thin bread on a piki stone
In an outdoor adobe oven,
Matrons in loose hairdos,
Maidens in elaborate butterfly hairdos.
One is in a Butterfly Kachina dance,
A decorative tableta on her head
And a pahos of feathers in her hand.
Her father weaves a white cotton
Mantel for her wedding,
An elder celebrates the birth of her baby,
Sprinkles a line of corn on the ground,
The father hunts for a rabbit skin
To put his baby in.

In the century-old painting,
"Moqui Arizona," by Kate T. Cory,
That I look at across my living room,
A Hopi woman with baby slung on her back
Picks sage at sunrise – or is it sunset –
As a glowing pastel-red-gold sun
Comes from around a mesa.
In childhood dreams of dark fears it rose,
Drew me to its warmth and wonder
To comfort me, and still does.

Spirit

Master craftsman of the sax,
Joel plays any style from jazz to
Perfect renditions of Ravel,
And, when he plays nostalgic tunes –
"Mood Indigo," "Body and Soul" –
Makes me want to sing along
And commune in the spirit.

Nate strikes his hands on a tabla
In crisp, complex rhythms,
Or his moon drum, or a conga
In gut-gratifying resonance,
The sounds of India, Africa, Wabanaki,
And makes me want to dance along
And join in the spirit.

Michael plays his Steinway,
With an uncanny insight into
The core of the composers –
Chopin, Debussy, Bartok.
I crave to sing again
His own chorales and cantatas.
The music is alive, it inspires me,
Merges its spirit with mine,
And we are as one spirit.

Dancing is divine.
Sufi dancers and Shakers like
Ballet and belly dancers
Strive for technique.
Flamenco and break-dancers
Contest with zest.
Square and round dancers
Socialize and laugh –
All are equally spiritual.

The same spirit that drives the dancer
Drives the skateboarder.
Isaac reached for the sky in
A spectacular move of "shredding",
And fell hard onto the sidewalk.
He tried again and again
Until he could land upright,
Skateboard and all, and roll on.
All are of one spirit.

Like shoots that push up in spring
Through earth and snow-cover
To seek the light and sustenance;
Like rhizomes and roots underground
That know in what direction to crawl;

Like birds that sense which sticks and straws
To pick for their nests,
And what songs to sing for a mate;
They all join in the spirit
That makes all things come alive,
Art and movement,
Life is the spirit.

Mysterious Openings

It is a very early memory and
I am in the bathtub.
"Come up and see the baby,"
My Mother exclaims to her guests,
"She's taking a bath!"
The women's coos
Glide past her and encircle
The little object trapped in the tub.
I have become a doll in
Collector's-item glory.
I clutch the washcloth for security
And wait.
It is important to be polite.
If I cooperate and allow myself
To be on display,
Maybe they will disappear.
The women at last titter away.
I am left in lukewarm water
But in solitary comfort.

Now in elementary school at recess
I am on the schoolyard
Off by myself.
I watch a gardener on a ladder up a tree
As he plasters over the tree's wound.
I'm drawn to the sky,

Looking up at it intensely,
Struck by an awareness that
I am not the centre of the universe,
That there is an existence
Outside my small self.
Have I just discovered that
The moon can be seen in the daytime?
Did the gardener wax philosophic
And humour me with earthy wisdom?
I am left to wonder in a lifetime of
Mysterious openings.

Meeting Together

Quakers and Wabanaki from the
Bay of Fundy-Gulf of Maine bioregion,
An Inuit woman from Labrador, an Innu chief,
An aged crone, a nursing baby,
A Haida man out on parole,
A feminist theologian from New Zealand,
An African man and Caribbean woman all
Sit on a hillside, around a fire pit,
In silence, but for the crackling fire and
The snuffle of a horse at the fence.

A kestrel settles on a wire as the
Elder extracts an eagle feather
From his sacred bundle and
Fans the smouldering end of
A sweetgrass braid for smudging.
I bathe my head, hands, and body
In the aromatic smoke and
Am renewed.

He tosses tobacco into the fire,
Offers a pinch of it to each of us
To do the same, saying
It will rise in the smoke to the Creator
Who will answer a prayer.

We all have the resources we need
If we look within and realize our
Instructions from the Creator, he tells us.
All natural things are connected,
Spiritually rooted in the direct existence
Of the Creator, the Life Force.
The web of life harbours spirit.
Together, he says, we can build an alliance
Of indigenous and non-indigenous people
Working for peace, justice and
Right relationship with Mother Earth.

"Meet together and know one another in
That which is eternal, which was
Before the world was,"
Advised George Fox at the
Founding of Quakerism in 1656.

A bowl of water is offered to
Our group of many ethnic origins
To sip and to share our dreams.
When the Talking Stick is passed around,
Allowing us to speak our thoughts,
To learn and empathize with the speaker,
I sense a common vision,
A confluence of spirit,
An emergence out of ethnic borders.

Around steaming pots of tea –
A centrepiece of new and old friends –
We share the potluck of
Dishes from diverse cultures, and
Traditional Wabanaki meals of
Succulent moose meat, salmon,
Corn, bean soup and bannock.
We compare our joys and sorrows
As we wash dishes together.
Michael joins the drummers and
Chanters around the big drum.

As we hunker down in our tent,
Crickets sing and pigs shuffle in their pen.
Impressions of the day settle in my mind –
A Maliseet woman chuckling at my
Inexperience with the sound of pigs;
Her sister-like teasing warmed me.

At first light, before the rooster's reveille,
Constellations fade,
Figures lose their silhouette quality,
A Quaker man passing our tent plays
Soft songs on his French horn to awaken us, and
The elder heralds us with his little bone flute
To re-join the circle of unifying prayers
Around the fire pit.

"Meet together and know one another in
That which is eternal, which was
Before the world was."

Ram Island Memories

Morning on Ram Island

As I lie in my camp bed
On the West Side of the island.
The sun filtering through the trees,
In a time between sleeping and waking,
I dream of trying to find a boat
To get over to my island.

Through my laze a motor rumbles,
Chuckles, like a man with laryngitis.
A lobsterman idles while he hauls his trap,
Picks out a lobster,
Checks it with his lobster ruler,
Tosses it over the gunwale.
Companions to the lobsterman,
The gulls quarrel about who's going to catch it,
Whine and whirl about the boat,
Alert to rejects or pieces of bait
And cackle at the contest.
We laugh at their theatre.

The sun starts to warm the air,
I must go to greet it on the East Side,
See if the loon I heard last night is around.
I must also have some coffee and
Pick up kindling on the way back –
Fir cones, rusty branches, birchbark.

Michael has gone off with his binoculars
To see the seals at North End.
Firewood and matches did not dampen overnight.
I hurry to start a fire before
He comes back and tries to outdo me.

My hearty fire boils the blue enamel kettle.
I peel an orange.
Two red squirrels quarrel.
An Acadian sparrow sings.
I scrub the grille in the Bay sand
And purify it over the flames.

Michael returns and reports on an eagle overhead
And seals sunning on their rocks.
We breakfast on coffee and grilled toast, then
Head for South End to see if the osprey
Has returned and built a new nest, and
If the clear water reveals sea urchins.

Osprey

On my way to a tiny cove
Just deep enough for
A high-tide bath,
An osprey pesters me for
My gleaming Ivory soap.

Cheep-cheep-cheep! it shrieks,
Targeting the counterfeit fish,
Swooping down, flapping frantic wings.
Will it alight on my hand or head
To snatch the supposed prey?

This theatre is repeated as I
Plunge into the cove, the soap now
Coated with a chalky saltwater film.
Defeated, the osprey shoots up to its
Nest high atop a fir tree.

Eaglets

Two adult-size eaglets
Yet still in the nest,
Screech at my approach.
Am I a threat
Or a food supplier
For their helpless hunger?

I muse, whose island is this?
Is it theirs when
There are no people here?
Is it theirs more than
The gulls and crows,
Seals, and salamanders?

Is it ours, a human family
Who built cabins on it and
Chop up trees for campfires?
They squeal their hungry plaint as
The parent eagle comes with prey
For their eager maws.

At last comes silence,
Only the sound of
A scolding red squirrel,
A scuffling mouse,
A luffing sail,
A purring motor.

Herons

In the strait between our island
And the next one
They stand in low tide
Like random stalks of grass,
Great blue herons concentrate on
Their target fish.

With cautious, slow-paced steps,
Svelte bodies are poised as
They look under the surface and
With eager, arched necks, suddenly
Thrust their long sharp bills into the deep
To spear their prey.

They once occupied the islands
And chattered at daybreak and dusk,
Almost smothering our attempts to sleep.
Now, a heron is a surprise.

In my tent, tucked in and adrift in sleep,
A heron grunts somewhere above me as the
Chicks vie for space in their nest.
One moves and awakens another and soon
The nestlings squawk in rhythmic, guttural cries,
Like a Balinese monkey chant.
They seem to be immediately overhead,
Is the nest secure in the tree?

In my half-dream state, I worry.
Will the mama heron tip out of the nest?
Will she plummet, her beak piercing the fabric
Of the tent and hit my face?
As soon as I recapture some sleep,
They start their squabbling again,
Continuing the cycle until daybreak, when,
Sleep deprived, I am almost glad to rise and recover in
Naps through the day on the beach,
On beds of lichen, and conifer needles.

As I lie on the North End beach,
A heron's rough rallying cry startles me,
Arouses me to grab binoculars as I hear the
Great wings audibly flap in
The deliberate way of the heron.
It takes flight from a tall fir,
wide powerful swoops,
Transporting its body, elongated
From talon to beak point,
And soars over the island and bay.

Bay Blast

In my sleeping bag, on our island,
In the middle of the dark and
Dense fog,
I am dimly conscious of
A distant sound on the Bay.

A sort of bleating punctuates
The muffled thrum of
A heavy ship as it crawls along
In the direction of my island –
An oil tanker in the deep Bay.

Its engine throbs steadily,
Making the waves hiss.
Abruptly, its foghorn bellows,
Like the Beanstalk Giant waking up for
An Englishman's blood and bones.

The sound echoes, the ship chugs,
Parting shushing waves, and again
Honks a monstrous horn.
The motor's drone vibrates through
My tensed body.

I now hear the wake splash,
The horn's glorious blast resounds
All over the Bay.
Gustav Mahler could not have
Bested its magnitude.

The ship passes at last,
The force of its presence
begins to diminish and lets me
Settle down, satisfied,
Before first light.

Dedications

Big Bang Theory

for Michael on his 83rd birthday

My big bang theory is that
My meaningful life began when I met you,
As if a fairy godmother
Touched me with her wand.
Suddenly, a miracle in a moment,
A marigold unfolded its golden petals,
A figure skater sprang up and spun
His spectacular axels,
Your pause in the Chopin Prelude
Was pregnant, just as Chopin intended.
My life with you has been a renaissance
Of new mysteries and meaning,
In a half-century continuum.

As the Big Bang developed land and sea,
Plant and animal life,
So it did our life together.
Like a jigsaw puzzle,
Pieces gradually fit together and made sense
But still reveal new scenes,
As we seek new ones.

How many times will the sparrow
Sing the same theme,
Will the cat curl up in my secure lap

Or venture outdoors into wet bushes?
In what modes will our sons
Compose their music?
In what styles will our granddaughters
Fashion their hair and high-heels?
Are the answers in the next puzzle move?

Our life is always an adventure,
While retaining the same devotion
To each other we had at the beginning –
Fifty-plus years of family lore and laughter,
In-house jokes and language,

Pronouncing words in the endearing way
A son did when he was learning it,
And grins only understood by us –
Memory etchings, bindings.

I give many thanks to the Creator,
The Force, the Spirit, for creating
The Big Bang for us
On that instant when we met.
I am thankful every day.
Yippee, Halleluiah, and Amen!

Different Strokes

*for Deanna and Andrew on their wedding,
October 12, 2013*

Someone once said that
art and music are
different languages for
expressing the same thing.

The couple love to explore the harbour,
they walk together
breakwater rocks and
shell-spangled beach as
seabirds chuckle above.

Amid a rock-adorned table stands
Deanna's bronze unicorn,
her gulls flutter across a wall and
halt as if waiting for companions
to complete the mural.

Across his bass Andrew brushes the bow.
He can caress the strings,
Smooth like honey over resonant wood,
or he can strangle them,
like a lemon puckering the lip.

She brushes paint on her canvases:
a windrow of eelgrass glitters with sand,
a veil of mist curls across
a palette of hot colours,
roses cluster on a mosaic backsplash.

He leaps from low to high notes
and makes a perfect landing in tune.
He scratches them like sand, then waves them;
slaps the wood and snaps the strings,
then graces them with a tender bow.

One wields a paintbrush,
the other, a bass bow.
Different strokes by ear and by eye
together create a new language.

For Liv, At Ten Months

A poppy unfurls wide, fiery scarlet petals.
A bead of rainwater twinkles from
The throat of a huge hosta plant.

Bitter meets sweet in Billie Holiday's song.
A shooting star streaks a clean arc, and
A dancer stretches her jeté to a new height.

A new life is created: it is Liv.
Dainty as a Dresden doll, her hair a copper tint,
Her soft cheeks sparkle with water from happy bath play.

Delicate meets sturdy, as she explores,
Crawls a zigzag path, stands and attempts a step.
Reenacting an ancient quest.

> *granddaughter Liv Kathleen Miller,*
> *born August 12, 2010*

Six Elegies For Isaac

Isaac William Miller, grandson, 1999-2014

1

Once when Isaac was just old enough – 2 ½ or 3 –
to form sentences, at Wilmot Park
He climbed the playground apparatus just up to
a pass-through tube, where he balked, saying,
"But what's on the other side?"

Later on, he loved debating,
tasting a phrase, *carpe diem,* sexism,
Quaker games and workshops,
expanding his mind.

He was always singing and improvising
lyrics to standard songs – and in tune.
He even allowed me to hear him sing
songs from "Fiddler on the Roof."

The image and soul of his vibrant, radiant
presence is almost tangible,
that I feel can overcome its absence.
I believe in what Tennyson said,

I hold it true whate'er befall:
I feel it, when sorrow most;
'Tis better to have loved and lost
Than never to have loved at all.

2

Isaac's first words after "Mama" and "Dada"
Were "vacuum cleaner" and "waffle maker."
He improvised with words,
Sprinkled his speech with
Isaac-speak, motifs,
Originally used words every few weeks,
Inserted into sentences.

Something would make him exclaim
"Amish!" in unexpected times,
"Word," proclaimed perhaps like an amen.
"Elbow!" as a long favourite,
As he loved stroking the texture of elbows,
Then he worked the word into familiar melodies.

At last came "Puma!"
The origin uncertain,
Revitalized it too into a rhythm,
Danced it at family reunions,
Shared his exuberance with all,
Even with me, his grandmother.
And then took it as a nickname.

Isaac, you are now a dream,
Like my most cherished ones
That return repeatedly.
Your dancing and singing

Are linked to mine;
Your skateboarding flights,
To my flying dreams.

In a repeated dream I had as a child
When I confronted a tall wall of a thicket,
I feared for the unknown on the other side,
But passed through into a glowing, rainbow-hued land.
If I can suspend the image in my mind over and over,
I can in reality suspend my love;
And it will not go away.

3

My sweet grandson lay in the coffin,
Dressed in a new white shirt,
Hands carefully placed one over the other,
Hair, just cut by the barber,
Soft on the white pillow,
Skin almost as white.
I gazed at him, talked to him,
His eyes seemed to open, lambent,
Eyelashes to flutter,
But when I bent over and kissed him,
His skin wouldn't move;
It was hard and cold.
I thought of an angel.
Why, this image from a pantheist
Of an angel?
But maybe this is what an angel is:
A beloved one stopped
In innocent youth,
His presence aloft
In loved-one's minds.

Especially in that of his father, my son
Who mourns him daily.
And I mourn my son.
Can the grief for grandson and son
Be quantified?

Is my sorrow more or less pungent
Than that of other grievers?
I have to bear my son's sorrow
And blot some of it off him.
He was *my little boy* just as
My grandson was my son's.
I guess my son is my best memento
Of my grandson,
And when he cries in grief,
I can share it,
I can cry for him too.

4

A crow swooped down to the porch,
Swept up sparrows,
Flourished sleek black wings
That became luminous blue in the sun,
Dazzled me through the glass door –
Like a flash of life.

Like the spark in Isaac,
As he spun his skateboard in the air
And zeroed down
To a square, crisp landing.
And the crow graced my grief –
Like a spirit sign.

5

At the convenience store
With his buddies after school,
At around nine years old,
Isaac held a skateboard in one hand
And a licorice strip in the other.
He introduced me to his friends,
Not just to be polite;
It was in his nature,
Unlike many callow kids.
This is how Isaac was.

The rush-hour traffic streamed and
A youth wanted to cross,
His look expectant and a leg on the curb.
He resembled Isaac,
A raw fourteen-year old
With hair to the shoulders,
And I stopped to let him go.
He thanked me with a little grin
And a wag of his hand.
This is what Isaac would have done.

6

It's January, two years since
He left us.
On a frosted branch
A lone leaf remains,
Swiveling on its stem,
Revealing a spark of
Isaac's soul,
Somehow tenaciously alive.
As wisps of snow
Are sifted from the branch,
I shed tears of memory.

Notes

"Eight Crow Impressions." Writing the first "Impression" was the start of my desire to write my thoughts in poem form as a change from the non-fiction I have usually written. In 1993 I was sitting in a Friend's living room in Quaker Meeting when a crow outside the window captured my attention. "Impression 2" was inspired by my Uncle Ted. When I was a child visiting my great aunt and uncle's summer cottage in Maine, Ted passed by the window stalking crows with his rifle. More "Impressions" followed into the 2010s.

"Crow Impressions" received second place in the Writers' Federation of New Brunswick's literary competition, 2009.

"Crow Impressions 1-3" were published in "Canadian Friend," August 1997.

"Crow Impressions 4," "Pigeons," and "Hard Hats" were set to music for a cappella choir by Michael R. Miller, 2008.

"Cock Pheasant" was inspired by a siting from my bedroom window when we lived near the Tantramar Marsh. This is another poem that writer and poet Harry Thurston critiqued for me. For payment he agreed to let me take him out to lunch.

"Cock Pheasant" received second place in the Writers' Federation of New Brunswick's literary competition, 2006.

"Turtle," refers to "Blackie," a red-ear pond slider who is more than a quarter of a century in age. She resides at our bay window in the cold months and out on our porch in the warm ones.

"Cat Haiku" could be applied to any of the cats we have had and loved: Robert, Zoe, or Zsazsa.

"Toad," my first poem, was written at age seven. It was printed in the yearbook of the Greenwich Academy, Greenwich, Connecticut, which I attended from kindergarten through grade three.

The "sidewalk philosopher" in "Barber Shop," was a man in Sackville, New Brunswick, much revered for befriending and doing chores for shopkeepers on Bridge Street. In fact, on his death his admirers got together and commissioned a sculpture representing his activities, which now stands on the corner of Bridge and Main Streets.

"Barber Shop" was published in *Poems From the Journey*, Canadian Quaker Pamphlet # 65, 2007.

"QWERTY, With Certainty" harkens back to my mother's typewriter, which was the first one I typed on, at around seven years of age, followed by the generations of typing devices developed since. Strangely enough, I am now almost as slow typing on my iMac remote-control keyboard as I was on that early 20th-century desktop typewriter. A bit unsettling, when I remember being a topnotch typist and compositor.

"Pan's Pipes" were in Point de Bute, New Brunswick, ten kilometres north of Sackville.

"Waterways" includes the experience of six different aquatic environments: "The Brook" runs through the property where I grew up until I was nine, in Greenwich, Connecticut; "The Ocean" can be the Atlantic or the Pacific, but especially Jones Beach and Fire Island off Long Island, New York, the New Jersey shore, and the beaches of Prince Edward Island and Nova Scotia;

"Long Island Sound" is from where my paternal grandparents lived, on the Sound in Rye, New York; "Quarry Pool" is from near Pompton Lakes, New Jersey. "The Tidal Bore" is from the Shubenacadie River at Maitland, Nova Scotia; "The Tantramar" is from the marshland region between Amherst, Nova Scotia and Sackville, New Brunswick where I lived from 1967 to 1999.

"Fundy Enigma" is set at the Cumberland Basin between New Brunswick and Nova Scotia.

"Moqui Arizona" is an oil painting by Kate T. Cory, an artist and suffragist friend of my grandmother, Lucy Cate Abercrombie. Cory lived with the Hopi from 1906 to 1912, painting and photographing them. I remember Cory's visiting my grandmother when she lived with us in the 1940s. This painting belonged to my grandmother and then came to me. Cory later designed the beautiful Smoki Museum for Native American artifacts in Prescott, Arizona. Michael and I traveled to Arizona in 2003 and 2008.

"Six Links To the Past" includes six settings: Link 1 is from the United States Southwest; Link 2 is from Hopedale, Labrador; Link 3 is from Kings Landing, New Brunswick; Link 4 is from Rye, New York; Link 5 is from Little Falls, New Jersey, a few miles from Montclair, where I lived in the 1940s and 50s; Link 6 is from Perry Street in West Village, Manhattan, NYC.

"Meeting Together" draws on six or seven gatherings Michael and I attended from 1989-1994 organized by alliance-building groups in Maine and New Brunswick.

"Ram Island Memories" are set on this five-acre family island in Penobscot Bay, Maine.

"Different Strokes" was written for my son Andrew's marriage to Deanna Musgrave on October 12, 2013, in The Sanctuary Theatre, Saint John, New Brunswick.

"For Liv" was written for my granddaughter, daughter of son Joel and Christine Jensen, on the occasion of her baptism in Ephraim Scott Memorial Church, a Presbyterian church in Montreal. The minister kindly gave the baptism in thanks for the ten years that Christine was the pianist and choir director of the church. Liv was ten months old (b. August 12, 2010).

"Six Elegies for Isaac" were written after the death of my grandson, Isaac William Miller, at the age of 14 (1999-2014). The first elegy was printed in the program at his funeral in Christ Church Cathedral, Fredericton, New Brunswick, on January l8, 2014. He is buried in Fredericton Rural Cemetery Extension.

About the Author

Edith Hoisington Miller was born in 1932 in Ossining, New York. After two years of liberal arts studies, she began working as a secretary in New York City, eventually in publishing with the McGraw-Hill Book Company, and as a freelance compositor for science books. Through her participation in choral groups she met and married organist, choirmaster, and composer, Michael R. Miller. The Millers eventually settled in Sackville, New Brunswick, where Michael served as professor of music for thirty-two years at Mount Allison University. They now live in Fredericton, New Brunswick.

She has been active in a wide variety of community-based art organizations in Sackville and Fredericton. She has participated in choral singing, dancing, and creative writing programs, and has taught creative movement to children and adults. In addition, she has been involved in social justice work, including alliance building with First Nation communities. She wrote a biweekly column for the *Sackville Tribune-Post* on environmental, justice, and Indigenous Canadian issues. She has done publicity writing for arts organizations and has contributed articles on the arts, especially on dance, to various publications.

Edith Miller is a member of the Writers' Federation of New Brunswick, from which she has received awards for her nonfiction and poetry. She has also been a juried member of the Professional Writers Association of Canada. She is the mother of three sons, all of whom are musicians. The Millers are members of New Brunswick Monthly Meeting of the Religious Society of Friends (Quakers).